Needs and Approaches for Educators and Parents of Gifted Gay, Lesbian, Bisexual, and Transgender Students

Terence Paul Friedrichs, Teresa Ryan Manzella, Robert Seney

Cheryll M. Adams, Series Editor

Copyright © 2018, National Association for Gifted Children

ISBN: 978-0-692-97452-0

No part of this book may be reproduced, scanned, or distributed in any printed or electronic form without written permission.

National Association for Gifted Children
1331 H Street, NW, Suite 1001
Washington, DC 20005
202-785-4268
http://www.nagc.org

TABLE OF CONTENTS

Preface 1

Dedication 2

Introduction to Gifted GLBTQ Youth 3

Characteristics of Gifted GLBTQ Students 11

Curricular Opportunities for Gifted GLBTQ Students 17

Educational Approaches for Gifted GLBTQ Students 26

Parental Guidance of GLBTQ Gifted Students 31

Community Mentoring for GLBTQ Gifted Youth 40

Future Opportunities and Challenges 46

Resources for GLBTQ Youth 51

Endnotes 57

About the Authors 63

About the Editor 64

PREFACE

In the coming decades, it may seem strange to readers that this manuscript, published in 2017, was one of the first focused solely on gifted gay, lesbian, bisexual, transgender, and questioning (GLBTQ) youth. Perhaps the future may include a world of open sexual-minority students and their supportive allies, teachers, parents, and curricula. Ample community resources to supplement school efforts for these youth may also exist. However, today's GLBTQ youth face considerable rates of suicide attempts, school absences, sexual assault, and substance use. Educators and curricula are often forbidden from discussing GLBTQ youth.

Future viewers also may not fully understand, without some detailed study, the long journey that this book's sponsoring organization, the National Association for Gifted Children, has undertaken as it grew in appreciation of sexual-minority issues. NAGC has responded gradually but positively to GLBTQ-related inclusivity, trends, and generational changes within education and society as a whole.

We are most grateful for NAGC's growth and wish for its continued rapid progress of recent years. We encourage the continued honoring of this movement through education and support of all gifted children. There will always be fallow periods, for NAGC and other gifted education groups, and these groups will always need dedicated, constructive, risk-taking advocates to inspire them.

DEDICATION

We, the authors, are especially grateful for the important people in our own lives for supporting us as sexual minorities. These individuals, too, have withstood bias in lean times, have celebrated our successes, and have urged us onward toward our future accomplishments on GLBTQ and many other matters.

For all my students, whose journeys have been difficult and for all those who have supported them. Onward and upward! ~Bob Seney

For all of the kids—my own and those of other people—who have been on this journey with me and whose futures I hope this work touches and helps to improve. ~Teresa Manzella

For the queer children of the future: May they be aware of the night, and rejoice in the dawn. ~Terry Friedrichs

INTRODUCTION TO GIFTED GLBTQ YOUTH

Terry Friedrichs

Readers can better understand the needs of gifted gay, lesbian, bisexual, transgender, and questioning students—also called "GLBTQ" or "sexual-minority" youth—through learning about several essential elements. These aspects include: (a) definitions of gifted GLBTQ youth, (b) prominent GLBTQ adults' successes, (c) sexual-minority people's historical struggles, (d) contemporary gifted GLBTQ students, (e) barriers facing gifted GLBTQ youth, (f) challenges in addressing their needs, and (g) factors to assist growth and support.

Definitions of GLBTQ Youth

There are various everyday definitions of "G," "L," "B," "T," and "Q." "Gay," "lesbians," and "bisexuals" have become more strongly etched in Americans' minds since the publication of the interview-based studies of human sexuality researcher Alfred Kinsey and his colleagues.[1] In Kinsey's and many subsequent social scientists' surveys, interviews, and analyses, gay youth are males oriented mostly toward other males in their sexual attractions, behaviors, and/or self-acknowledged identities. Lesbians are females oriented primarily toward other females in their attractions, behaviors, and/or identities. And bisexuals are oriented substantially toward both genders.[2]

Transgender is a more contemporary term used by social scientists.[3] Transgender girls are born with male anatomy and identify as female, and transgender males are born with female anatomy and identify as male. Transgender youth may be attracted to either gender. However, they are perhaps best known for their boundary-crossing gender identities. Queer students, another recently-labeled group may be gay, lesbian, bisexual, or transgender, and are known for their unabashed "non-heterosexual" status.[4] Finally, questioning youth, another Q population, are often described by educators as uncertain of their sexual orientations.[5] These students' uncertainty is generally due to developmental reasons or cultural repression.

These increasingly numerous definitions for sexual minorities reflect sexually-diverse adults' and youths' efforts toward self-definition and self-determination, according to teachers and counselors who have worked directly with these youth.[6] Parents and community agencies have long noted that these motivations may prove challenging to some gifted GLBTQ youth who are particularly early or who are especially strong in their self-definitions.[7] Educators and parents need to be aware of how each group—and how each member within each group—self-identifies, so that they can most respectfully address that group.

We purposely use a variety of acronyms for GLBTQ youth throughout this publication, to honor how people identify themselves.

Prominent GLBTQ Adults' Successes

As illustrated in the well-respected publication *Lavender Lists*, there are those Americans who have met the definitions of "GLBTQ," and have excelled in one or more of the following domains mentioned in the federal definition of giftedness: intellectual and academic, physical and athletic, and physical and aesthetic.[8] Each domain is rich with individuals from diverse backgrounds.

Academics	Athletes	Artists	Leaders
Ruth Benedict (Anthropology)	Brian Boitano (Figure Skating)	James Baldwin (Writing)	Jane Addams (Social Reform)
Allan Bloom (Philosophy)	Jason Collins (Basketball)	John Cheever (Novelist)	Tammy Baldwin (Politics)
John Boswell (History)	Britney Greiner (Basketball)	Ellen DeGeneres (Comedy)	Malcolm Boyd (Religion)
Charlotte Bunch (Women's Studies)	Billie Jean King (Tennis)	Tom Ford (Fashion Designer)	Clive Davis (Business)
Lillian Faderman (history)	David Kopay (Football)	Audrey Lorde (Writing)	Andrea Dworkin (Women's Rights)
Edgar Z. Friedenberg (Sociologist)	Greg Louganis (Diving)	Kate Millett (Writing)	David Geffen (Business)
Paul Goodman (cultural statistics)	Martina Navratilova (Tennis)	Robert Rauschenberg (Painting)	Sonia Johnson (Religion)
Alfred Kinsey (Human Sexuality)	Diana Nyad (Swimmer)	Bessie Smith (Singing)	Harvey Milk (Politics)
Camille Paglia (Social Critic)	Robbie Rogers (Soccer)	Rita Mae Brown (Writing)	Bayard Rustin (Politics)
James Sears (Education)	Bill Tilden (Tennis)	Andy Warhol (painting)	Randi Weingarten (Unions)

Historical Struggles of Gifted GLBTQ People

The historical achievements of these and other such sexual-minority adults and youth are remarkable in light of the discrimination they faced, particularly in their own neighborhoods, churches, and families.[9] Well into the 1970s, GLBTQ adults rarely "came out" in the workplace, due to the likelihood that they could be fired because of their visibility about their sexual orientations. As described by GLBTQ studies scholar James Sears, gifted sexual-minority students, who might have been inspired by these historical figures' achievements, often were unaware of those attainments because of schools' silence on GLBTQ issues.[10] Due to this silence, these pupils had very few successful role models. Gifted sexual-minority youth have also had few pathways by which to stabilize and ensure their ongoing excellent performance. The students were pushed into compulsory shows of heterosexuality, sometimes engaging in cover-ups of their sexual orientations. For example, some young gay males who were not inclined toward football tried out for the sport anyway, to enhance their images as "strong." Other such males might date women to convey their "heterosexuality."

Gifted sexual-minority students "passed" as heterosexual with such approaches, even though they were aware of their sexual-orientation differences. Due to gifted GLBTQ youths' self-awareness, they sometimes suffered a loss of their self-esteem and a significant increase in their stress levels. Other gifted sexual-minority pupils, who were more open about their identities, were targeted for their GLBTQ-related differences. As charted since the 1980s, by national sexual-minority organizations, such as the Gay, Lesbian, and Straight Educators Network (GLSEN), the rate of verbal harassment of GLBTQ students consistently exceeded 80%. The rate of physical harassment for these same pupils exceeded 40%, and the rate of physical assault for these youth hovered around 30%. Though accurate violence-related statistics for transgender students are hard to find (due to the even greater discrimination that these youth faced), it was likely that rates of harassment and assault for transgender youth were higher than this already-high composite GLBTQ average for this period.[11] Sexual-minority youth strongly needed to engage in productive school activities to show their value to school and society. They also needed to monitor their safety—sometimes even needing to run for their lives. When faced with such external pressures, gifted sexual minorities often retreated within themselves, choosing to focus on homework or on extracurricular activities, unlike some other GLBTQ youth.[12]

Contemporary Gifted GLBTQ Students

Despite the challenges faced by sexual-minority youth and adults, America's sexual-minority rights movement accelerated beginning in the 1970s. Basic GLBT-rights laws—often encompassing employment, credit, and public accommodations, and sometimes education—began to be established across the United States, beginning with Wisconsin in 1982. By 2015, approximately half of all states have passed such laws. At the same time, numerous metropolitan and suburban districts required non-biased treatment of sexual-minority students in school.[13]

With the gradual coming out encouraged by supportive laws and by prominent, open GLBTQ people, more students began to self-identify as sexual minorities in the 1990's, especially the many gifted youth who believed in the moral imperative of coming out. Thereafter, these pupils' excellence became more noticed, both within and outside school. The largest study done directly with gifted GLBTQ teens found that 36% of their 53 subjects (26 boys and 27 girls) who were attendees of sexual-minority youth social- and-support groups in seven U.S. metropolitan areas, self-reported as being enrolled in gifted programs. Of these same 53 students, over 40% had won multiple creativity and/or leadership awards at school or in the community.[14] Over a decade later, another study found a similar level of giftedness (about 30%) among 1,000 surveyed members of sexual-minority adult groups along with very high rates of overexcitabilities, including intellectual, imaginational, as well as leadership abilities.[15]

Barriers Facing Gifted GLBTQ Youth

In spite of the multifaceted accomplishments of so many of today's GLBTQ youth, they still encounter barriers at school. According to GLSEN, many sexual-minority students continue to encounter verbal harassment rates of 70%, physical harassment rates of 40%, and physical assault rates of 20%. Transgender-student harassment and assault rates are even higher than those of the overall sexual-minority population.[16]

This bias continues partly because American states, cities, and school districts are still without protections for GLB and especially transgender adults and students.[17] Many students still live in fear of what will happen to them. On a more-subtle level, many GLBTQ youth continue to go through their school years without learning one positive thing about themselves. These pupils continue to lack essential self-knowledge with which to lead their lives, since most American curricula in literature, history, science, health, politics, and other areas still make no mention of sexual-minority people.[18] This quest for self-knowledge is especially important for gifted GLBTQ youth.[19]

Challenges in Addressing GLBTQ Youth Needs

Many school districts still have rules that teachers and students should not highlight GLBTQ topics in class.[20] This prohibition even extends to districts that claim to have outlawed sexual-minority discrimination. Both GLBTQ and straight students are prevented from acquiring desired knowledge about sexual-minority rights. Even when GLBTQ students and teachers have opportunities to speak up, they often do not take advantage of those opportunities, for fear that they may be perceived as "gay." That "gay" status may still marginalize these advocates significantly within their very conservative localities. Some states with so-called "No Promo Homo" laws, which prohibit education about or discussion of sexual minorities, go to great lengths to stem what they see as a rising tide of homosexuality. Acting in the spirit of restrictive state laws, school districts may purchase textbooks that altogether avoid "controversial" issues, such as sexual-minority rights. The federal government, a possible force for forward-moving classroom discussions and textbooks, is reticent to break the silence and tell states to devise GLBTQ curriculum. In the absence of direct GLBTQ-related discussions, gifted sexual and gender minorities feel challenged to break the deafening silence on these issues.[21]

If the federal government has been silent on curricular issues, it inspired hopes for transgender students with the passage of a 2016 Executive Order from President Obama requiring some safety and equity measures be taken for them.[22] Then, those hopes were tamped down with the 2017 rescinding of some of those measures by the Trump Administration.[23] It is fair to say that, at any given point in time, educators must be prepared to consider existing guidelines and laws for serving transgender and other LGBTQ students; however, they will always need to think most carefully about the most pressing needs of the sexual and gender minority youth whom they face each day. Those are the transcendent needs of all children for safety, humanity, and knowledge.

Factors to Assist Growth

While there remains reticence to push for GLBTQ-related curricular and instructional funding at the local, state, and national levels, there are trends that push for something more GLBTQ-positive than currently exists.[24] Districts have been strongly encouraged to establish rules for GLBTQ student safety because of federal court rulings in favor of harassment plaintiffs and because of the increasing number of state "safe schools" laws. Most U.S. districts have Gay-Straight Alliances (GSAs), which serve as focal points for sexual-minority and straight students gathering together. School districts have an increasing number of validated curricula from which to choose to teach straight and sexual-minority youth about sexual-minority topics. Finally, gifted sexual minorities may be especially active in organizing GSA's on pro-GLBTQ school safety rules.[25]

Conclusion

Definitions of "gifted GLBTQ" youth and descriptions of their successes, may provide a broader and more positive view of this population than had existed previously. Learning about these youths' historical struggles provides an appreciation of their social challenges. Discovering gifted sexual minorities' large numbers and contemporary struggles may inspire supportive action. And learning about both controversial and facilitative factors surrounding others' efforts for gifted GLBTQ youth may cause advocates to take decisive action on behalf of these students', devising appropriate curriculum and instruction, and effectively involving parents, mentors, and community resource professionals.

CHARACTERISTICS OF GIFTED GLBTQ STUDENTS

Terry Friedrichs

An examination of GLBTQ adults and sexual-minority students is needed. These include distinctive intellectual, academic, social, emotional, physical, and athletic needs. They are most-thoroughly documented in four multi-subject studies: (a) Peterson and Rischar's[26] interviews of college-aged gifted sexual-minority students who reflected back on their teen years, (b) Treat's[27] statistical analyses of 1,000 sexual-minority adult survey respondents (both gifted and non-gifted), also reflecting on their teen years, (c) Whittenburg's and Treat's[28] summary of surveyed similarities and differences between gifted GLBT students and other gifted youth, and (d) Friedrichs's four survey-and interview-based studies of male and female gay, lesbian, and bisexual youth.[29]

Peterson and Rischar comment mostly on shared male-and-female traits, while Treat, Whittenburg and Treat, and Friedrichs describe both shared and distinctive male and female traits. All researchers had a preponderance of lesbian, gay, and bisexual subjects, with few mentions of transgender youth. If these investigators' research were conducted today, with updated social contexts and different research tools and methodological techniques, they might well attain somewhat different results about what are similar and what are different traits within and between LGBT groups.[30] However, future researchers will still probably strive to find aggregated data that speaks to the common experiences of gifted LGBTQ youth, as well as distinctive information that characterizes separate groups. Through sets of updated data, we will continue to strive to serve these students as a whole, as well as the highly diverse groups within this population. With more openness among, and positive social focus on, transgender students, we hopefully will especially learn more about these youth. Until then, educators and parents can observe the many ways in which gifted transgender youth may be similar to, and different from, those high-potential LGB youth whom researchers have begun to address.[31]

Intellectual and Academic Traits

Gay and bisexual males and lesbian and bisexual females. Both gifted gay and bisexual males and gifted lesbian and bisexual females often have intellectual interests that the dominant culture views as "not gender-appropriate." Academically, these groups can feel discouraged from pursuing their true passions, but may later fight back against such discouragement and pursue those interests. Gifted sexual-minority boys and girls are distinctive from other GLBTQ youth in citing gifted education as providing an opportunity to support their explorations of GLBTQ studies, passions, and interests.[32]

Gay and bisexual males. High-potential male students frequently have an intellectual preference for cultural diversity in students, staff, and speakers. To facilitate their academic achievement, these young men wish for pro-gay community mentors and speakers. They also desire accelerated school programming so that they may move to more stimulating environments.[33]

Lesbian and bisexual females. These gifted females report being instinctive and inquisitive and having dreams and fantasies. They especially appreciate exploring unorthodox ideas, and enjoy exploring their own feelings through writing and discussions. In their scholastic endeavors, the girls, like the boys, wish to excel. They also appreciate each other's enriched coursework and being grouped with advanced peers, since they thrive on the academic comradery.[34]

Social/Emotional Traits

As with intellectual/academic characteristics, gifted gay, lesbian, and bisexual students' social/emotional traits may include those shared by males and females, those displayed just by males, and those showed just by females.[35]

Gay and bisexual males, and lesbian and bisexual females. Socially, both gifted and bisexual boys and gifted lesbian and bisexual girls often feel isolated from other youth. They may experience anti-GLBTQ hostility within school and often feel in danger. They may fear getting bullied more when they disclose their sexual orientations. Compared to general groups of sexual minorities, gifted GLBTQ students' perceptiveness about society's lack of concern for them, may drive them even further away from both educators and other authority figures. In fact, there are still more states that don't protect GLBTQ students than do protect them. In light of this reality, high-potential GLBTQ youth understandably desire safe spaces. Fortunately, things often get better for them in senior high school, since the coming-out process for senior high youth has become easier in recent years.[36]

Emotionally, both sexual-minority males and females may feel different from other youth. They may even be so small in numbers in their community, that they feel invisible, as they search with great difficulty for peers who are also gifted and gay. That sense of difference may result in introversion, depression, and even self-destructive behavior. With time, these youth often begin to piece together their sexual identities. They generally find persons to whom they are attracted, engage in sexual activities, and stabilize emotionally. As they come out, they share their differences with others, embrace their heightened sensitivities and strengths, and constructively share their psychological distress.[37]

Gay and bisexual males. Emotionally, these young men have desire discussion on human sexual behaviors. They value their friends who are sexual minorities. Despite their ardent desire for support from others for their differences, they also wish to seek happiness independently through their careers. They appreciate parents' introduction to gay role models, as well as counselors' demonstrations of GLBT support. Males wish for a more encompassing sense of social support than the one which they now experience, whether they are social isolates or popular students.[38]

Lesbian and bisexual females. These young women often wish to use their assertiveness to separate themselves from other girls and to reflect on their individual places in the social, academic, and career worlds. They like to learn about others' ideas, especially regarding social fairness. They may appreciate values-clarification and moral-reasoning exercises, information about others' feelings and values, and reflections on the values of traditional and non-traditional women's roles. They learn much from role models, especially lesbian ones.[39] Emotionally, young females prefer positive self-images and independence in peer relationships. They value others' positive mentions of sexual minorities and others' acceptance of their attractions to other girls. They seek information about sex and take the time to seek out positive relationships with peers and parents.[40]

Physical and Athletic Needs

There is less information about gifted GLBTQ youths' physical and athletic needs than about their intellectual, scholastic, social, and emotional needs. Yet, some important information can be reported about those needs.[41] These needs are important to address given many gifted students' significant but underemphasized potential in these area.[42]

Gay and bisexual males, and lesbian and bisexual females. There is no statistically-significant difference in psychomotor overexcitability between heterosexual groups and several sexual-minority groups (gays, lesbians, and bisexuals). However, these same sexual-minority groups have exceeded both heterosexual males and females in psychomotor functioning.[43]

Gay and bisexual males. In their physical development, these young men desire recreational outlets to release their physical energy and reduce their social frustration. Often, this release of energy comes in the arena of individual, rather than team, sports. The young men especially wish to get away from school pressures and tensions through their physical endeavors and (perhaps different from other GLBTQ students) to establish their own distinctive identities.[44]

Lesbian and bisexual females. Physically, these young women also need outlets for their pent-up energy resulting from the greater amount of social frustration that these youths can face, compared to other teens. Ample and varied recreational activities prove helpful for this purpose.[45]

Conclusion

As distinctive as gifted GLBTQ traits are, these characteristics may be less developed in environments with fewer stimulating learning materials, less supportive teaching and parenting techniques, and a lack of mentoring options.[46] Yet, even in the most oppressive settings, gifted GLBTQ traits are there for the uncovering.[47] When we examine those characteristics, we see many shared and some distinctive traits between groups. With knowledge of various gifted GLBTQ groups' similarities and differences, readers can better reach an understanding of these youth.

CURRICULAR OPPORTUNITIES FOR GIFTED GLBTQ STUDENTS

Bob Seney

Curricular opportunities can help GLBTQ students develop their strengths. In contemporary American schools, these opportunities fall into two major categories: (a) those meeting intellectual and academic needs, and (b) those addressing social and emotional needs. Intellectual needs entail an understanding of adolescent identity, differentiation of content and pedagogy, and GLBTQ—focused curricula. Social and emotional needs can be addressed through young adult literature and bibliotherapy as well as through research-based inquires.

Meeting Intellectual and Academic Needs

Gifted adolescents face many changes in their lives and deal with the classic adolescent milestones:

- Adjust to a new physical sense of self.
- Adjust to new intellectual abilities.
- Adjust to increased cognitive demands at school.
- Develop expanded verbal skills.
- Develop a personal sense of identity.
- Establish adult vocational goals.
- Establish emotional and psychological independence from his or her parents.
- Develop stable and productive peer relationships.
- Learn to manage her or his sexuality.
- Adopt a personal value system.

- Develop increased impulse control and behavioral maturity.[48]

There are also increased social and cultural pressures put upon contemporary adolescents. *"Today's young adults differ significantly from the individuals found in the 12- to 20-year-old age group 30 or 40 years ago. Contemporary adolescents develop faster."*[49] Smetana's, Compione-Barr's, and Metzger's article, "Adolescent Development in Interpersonal and Societal Contexts" in the *Annual Review of Psychology* is recommended for a review of classic studies in adolescent development.[50]

Gifted students face even more hurdles:

- Lack of appropriate academic challenge.
- Boredom in school.
- Bullying from non-gifted peers and even some teachers.
- Particular overexcitabilities.
- A feeling of not belonging.

These combined challenges can lead GLBTQ youth to feel overwhelmed.

Gifted students must be appropriately challenged academically and have their social/emotional needs met. In the classroom, this is sought through differentiation, enrichment, acceleration, and rigor.[51] The primary approach in most programs and classrooms appears to be the use of differentiation. While it is not the intent of this chapter to define or to defend this approach, it is important to realize that with the common and popular use of the term "differentiation," the concept has been reduced to "something different." This is not the original intent or the purpose of this strategy as it is used in gifted education. In earlier definitions, the concept of qualitative modification was most important. Differentiation sought to meet the individual needs, abilities, and interests of each gifted student. The tools of enrichment and acceleration are used to provide individual academic challenge and that differentiation for gifted students is different from general classroom differentiation.

"Differentiation for gifted students does not mean simply giving them more activities to do that the learner may see as "more of the same" (what we call "MOTS"). Instead, the content focuses on advanced concepts and complex ideas, and learners use strategies (step-by-step tasks) and thinking skills with greater degrees of sophistication. Indeed, these students should be using the tools of a practicing professional – a disciplinarian – to produce authentic products that have value to a real-world audience. This all takes place in an environment that builds students' intrinsic motivation to take on more responsibility for their own learning; that is, they become autonomous learners."[52]

Current brain research indicates that gifted students have more neural connectors in their frontal cortex than do typical learners. Thus, they are able to process information much more quickly, and make complex connections between ideas and thoughts.[53] Appropriate differentiation allows GLBTQ youth to participate in the social/political dialogue of society's sexually-divergent individuals, which is increasingly important for transgender individuals in current settings. Including topics on GLBTQ issues allows these students to see themselves in the curricula as well as meet their own needs. For example, differentiation of GLBTQ topics can be accomplished by having students take the role of an investigative reporter in researching societal attitudes towards the gay community. The learner will not only learn the skills of being an investigative reporter, but also will have an opportunity to view issues through the lens of a professional. Similarly, students can also gain a great deal by immersing themselves in the roles of sociologist, psychologist, politician, or any other profession of interest.[54]

This is not only curriculum designed for gifted students, but is curriculum that includes meeting the needs of sexual-minority persons. Working on strengths in GLBTQ-focused curricula takes many forms, but a primary approach is to use a research-based inquiry into these and other critical issues:

- The history of the gay movement in the U.S.
- The role, contributions of sexual-minority individuals to our historical and modern societies.
- U.S. political progress for GLBTQ individuals in basic civil rights, gay marriage, and military service. Recent political attacks on transgender individuals make this a relevant topic for investigation and research.
- Concerns about physical development and activity for GLBTQ students can be addressed by specifically focusing on the lives and contributions of gay athletes. This emphasis can help debunk the myth that GLBTQ individuals are not physically active and involved across a range of sports.

An excellent guideline for teachers to develop their own curriculum can be found in *Bridging the Gap: A Tool and Technique to Analyze and Evaluate Gifted Education Curricular Units*.[55] This article provides a checklist of 12 key features that differentiated curricula should meet; guidelines for developing and evaluating curricula, a rationale for exemplary and differentiated curricula for the gifted, a detailed description of the key features, and a rubric for evaluating differentiated curricula.

In terms of students' research-based inquiries into the roles and contributions of GLBTQ individuals, *Lavender Lists* can be an excellent resource. [56] It was noted earlier that GLBTQ youth value references and information on other sexual-minorities, especially successful sexual-minority individuals. Engaging in such studies can lead directly to fulfillment of their social and emotional needs. Perhaps one of the most important recent developments in gifted education is recognizing the importance of meeting the social and emotional needs of gifted learners.[57] Meeting these social/emotional needs must be a priority. This is especially significant for transgender students, for whom acceptance and emotional support is crucial.

Meeting Social and Emotional Needs

Gifted individuals not only think differently from their peers, they also feel differently.[58] The link between emotion and cognition is now recognized in the research literature. [59]

"The picture of the more emotional person, as it is emerging from this research, stands in significant contrast to the traditional dominant view. This picture reveals that a high level of emotional responsiveness may be associated with advanced cognitive organization."[60]

"Giftedness is the capacity for high abstract reasoning and greater awareness. It bestows on its bearer overexcitability, intensity, complexity, and idealism. The complexity of gifted minds is mirrored in the complexity of their emotions. These individuals tend to be emotionally sensitive, empathic, compassionate; they have a difficult time accepting criticisms, and they often feel isolated and misunderstood. They need therapists who can deal with their complexity and intensity." [61]

With this understanding of giftedness and with the additional emotional conflicts that often surround GLBTQ individuals, it is critically important to support and nurture these social-emotional needs. Several strategies are readily available, and are built upon recognized strengths of gifted learners. One of these strengths is their interest in reading. Quite often, reading becomes a coping strategy to deal with a world that is often hostile to gifted individuals, especially gifted GLBTQ students. Literature in problem-based learning, studying through thematic issues, and exploring bibliotherapy are also reliable strategies. Literature, especially young adult literature, provides a very rich resource for investigating and developing social and emotional issues.

The strategy of bibliotherapy is quite useful in this area. Briefly, bibliotherapy is a technique of having students read about individuals in literature who may have similar problems to themselves.[62] It is a counseling technique adapted for classroom use. By reading about the problem or issue, the problem is "defused," and this defusion helps students to realize that others have the same problems as they do. They are not alone, which is the first and perhaps the most important step in effectively dealing with challenges. The term "therapeutic reading" or "developmental reading" is sometimes interchanged for bibliotherapy.[63]

There are many resources available to guide teachers, counselors, and/or parents in using bibliotherapy. Two excellent resources are *Bibliotherapy: The Interactive Process* by Arlene McCarty Hynes & Mary Hynes-Berry, and *Bibliotherapy: When Kids Need Books: A Guide for Those in Need of Reassurance and their Teachers, Parents, and Friends* by Amy Recob, which includes over 50 current issues that face youth today, with recommended books to use to address the targeted concerns. One important example is

Beautiful Music for Ugly Children by Kirstin Cronn-Mills, which centers on a teen transgender protagonist.

Another important resource for both bibliotherapy and finding related literature for recommended reading and classroom study is the American Library Association's (ALA) Stonewall Award Books, otherwise known as The Mike Morgan & Larry Romans Children's & Young Adult Literature Award. Since 2010, ALA has named as Stonewall Award winners those books for children and young adults that address GLBTQ issues. The lists of past award recipients and ALA's other sexual-minority-related Honor Books are helpful.

These books vary in the manner in which they deal with GLBTQ issues. Some directly and honestly approach relationships, and others are more subtle. As an example of a more subtle treatment, *I'll Give You the Sun* by Jandy Nelson, also a 2015 Printz Award Winner, deals with the broken trust between paternal twins. However, as a subtheme, the brother is learning to deal with his growing attraction to and relationship with the boy who lives next door. On the other hand, David Leviathan's *Boy Meets Boy* deals directly with the issues of coming out. One of the 2017 Honor Books, *Pride: Celebrating Diversity & Community* by Robin Stevenson is nonfiction and deals with the history and development of gay pride.

Bibliotherapy readily can introduce philosophical questions and ultimately the study of philosophy. For younger students, Matthew Lipman's *Philosophy for Children* program is appropriate. It uses literature to illustrate major world philosophies and philosophical ideas without naming the philosophers themselves. For older students, especially if Lipman's series has been completed, *A History of Western Philosophy* by Bertrand Russell identifies philosophers by name.

What is suggested here is that GLBTQ-sensitive curricula not only inform all students on sexual- minority issues, but they also create understanding and empathy, allowing gifted GLBTQ learners to find a more comfortable stance in the emerging pro-GLBTQ world.[64] As they relate their skills and interests to pertinent, realistic, and relevant curricula, gifted sexual- minority students will discover a better understanding of self and will build greater self- acceptance. They will become equipped to take a place in creating a better, more sensitive world.

The National Association for Gifted Children's (NAGC) Positon Statement "Supporting Gifted Students with Diverse Sexual Orientation and Gender Identities" states, *"Whether engaged in academic, affective, or career programming, educators dealing with gifted GLBT students must model openness, fairness, and sensitivity regarding sexual- orientation issues."* [65] In addition, the NAGC Position Statement "Nurturing Social and Emotional Development of Gifted Children" emphasizes the importance of supporting the social-emotional growth of gifted students.[66]

Conclusion

The academic and social-emotional needs of GLBTQ students can be met through appropriate, challenging curriculum that provides positive sexual-minority role models, that utilize strategies and resources that speak to their needs, and that appreciates the sensitivities, intensities, and interests of gifted GLBTQ youth. Educators and parents must work together to devise appropriately creative curricular content and instructional strategies. These efforts can inform both students and adults themselves, as these adults meet the unique needs of GLBTQ youth. This chapter's strategies provide a good starting point for curriculum creation in accepting and nurturing environments in which today's gifted students can succeed.

EDUCATIONAL APPROACHES FOR GIFTED GLBTQ STUDENTS

Terry Friedrichs

Gifted gay and bisexual males, and gifted lesbian and bisexual females, have similarities in their needs, they also display differences. These needs may change over time, in response to differing contexts and the fluidity of sexual orientations, gender identities, and giftedness. As the needs of gifted transgender youth become more thoroughly researched, there should be a much-needed increase in the number and variety of empirically-based approaches to teach these pupils.[67] These approaches will help bolster the current, experientially-based recommendations of transgender advocacy organizations and state educational authorities.

Intellectual and Academic Needs

An evolving picture of helpful intellectual and scholastic approaches emerges from school-focused surveys and interviews done with current gifted-GLBTQ teens,[68] as well as from surveys and interviews conducted with gifted sexual-minority adults looking back on their teen years.[69] From an intellectual standpoint, since gifted gay and bisexual (GB) males express appreciation of diversity in their texts and speakers, educators can provide these young men with increasingly specialized GLBTQ-focused curricula and independent studies. These English curricula may include GLBTQ focused journaling and modules in health on GLBTQ sexuality, smoking, substance-abuse, and HIV/AIDS. High-potential lesbian and bisexual (LB) females can benefit from GLBTQ mentors who communicate in the youths' same language, and from educators who can find these mentors at ever-more-present GLBTQ community centers. The young women can also benefit from sexual-minority and straight educators who challenge sexual-minority stereotypes in student discussions. These women can benefit from teacher responses to GLBTQ-themed journaling from personalized encouragement, connections to skilled mentors at community centers, and from teachers in all subjects who challenge GLBTQ stereotypes. Gifted transgender students especially may appreciate the challenging of gender and other stereotypes and may appreciate the opportunity to exchange views with other transgender youth and adults.[70]

Academically. Educators can encourage high-potential GB males to work with GLBTQ-sensitive mentors on advanced goals. These young men can also be accelerated, based on their academic proficiencies and safety needs. Educators might know of well-placed GLBTQ mentors in business and industry who can encourage strong student performance. They also might know of places where these young men can ply their skills, openly and proudly, as gays and bisexuals. These educators might also be well situated to know where acceleration of young GB males can be done at strong academic institutions that are also safe. (Strong academic institutions are not always the safest.) Similarly, teachers and counselors group gifted LB females with similarly-achieving female and male peers. These educators can be aware of successes of achieving females and motivational sets that help them achieve. They might also know of places where supportive, high-achieving females gather. High-potential transgender students, striving to do their best academically, can particularly benefit from safe and supportive mentors, internships, schools, and other educational meeting places.[71]

Social and Emotional Needs

Through their active work with individuals and groups of gifted sexual minorities, educators can make a difference in these students' social and emotional, as well as academic, lives. Gifted gay and bisexual males very much appreciate teachers' social support. These young men appreciate inclusive classroom language that treats sexual minorities and straights equally.[72] These males also appreciate educators who support GLBTQ youth as school leaders. Supportive educators can navigate GB males to positions of authority within schools or within community or state organizations (such as roles on student councils, community boards, or state legislative page teams). High-potential lesbian and bisexual females enjoy time spent, both by themselves and with a teacher, in working out the student's value systems.[73] They also enjoy learning, both in social studies and literature classes, about others' feelings, including the feelings of lesbian role models. These girls appreciate values clarification and moral reasoning exercises, through which they can develop their personal systems of fairness. These young women also value individualized guidelines, so that they can function more independently in academic settings. The need for transgender-specific inclusive language, role models, and leadership opportunities can be especially important to transgender youth.[74]

Emotional perspective. Educators can effectively tap the individual interests of high-potential GB males in planned lessons and ad-hoc discussions about homosexuality, bisexuality, and other human sexual-behavior patterns.[75] Educators can especially encourage broadened friendship circles that include sexual minorities. GLBTQ role models, from school, community, or the news, can be identified for sexual-minority youth. By consulting these channels, young men can find their own paths to personal and professional happiness. Educators can also work actively with gifted LB females to develop more-positive self-images, an important endeavor when self-esteem for these youth may have been challenged in the contextual homophobia they may face.[76] Teachers and counselors can help enhance self-images through their mentions of these young women's (and other sexual minorities') past accomplishments. These girls may also appreciate independence training for college, career, and other life decisions. High-potential LB females look forward to teachers' open commentary with a non-judgmental attitude about the existence of same-sex relationships. These youth also appreciate constructive relationships with their parents and educators, including specific affirmation from these adults for being sexual minorities. Educators can assist transgender students through knowledgeable comments about the transgender community, through attention to these youths' self-image, and through support of these students' plans for creative career paths. [77]

Physical and Athletic Needs

Gifted gay and bisexual male youth benefit physically from educators' arrangement and affirmation of diversified recreational opportunities, which may be tailored to the students' specific physical needs.[78] According to these youth, these opportunities enable them to release energy and defuse social frustrations. Some young men prefer individual recreational activities, such as swimming or martial arts, while others prefer supportive team activities. High-potential lesbian and bisexual females particularly desire varied athletic outlets, including those calling for sheer strength as well as those requiring precision. High-potential transgender students can perform in outstanding fashion when they have access to safe locker rooms, to teams that fit their gender identity, and to coaches and players who cheer them on in their quest for excellence.[79]

Conclusion

Teachers and counselors can assist gifted GLBTQ students in all major student-need areas. Workable, detailed approaches range from long-practiced solutions, such as academic acceleration for accomplished GLBTQ students, to innovative approaches, such as providing students with individualized paths toward physical growth. Many approaches, if supported by parents, mentors, and community members with an eye toward the individual desires of the student, can support young male and female sexual minority students.

PARENTAL GUIDANCE OF GLBTQ GIFTED STUDENTS

Teresa Manzella

Parenting, like teaching, is a challenging task. Parenting gifted children brings on additional layers of challenges, as these children typically need more effort providing advocacy at school, coping with overexcitabilities in everyday life, and delivering almost constant intellectual stimulation.

When children belong to multiple marginalized groups—gifted, GLBTQ, and possibly another sexual minority (agender, intersex, or asexual)—parents often find themselves faced with seemingly unanswerable questions. These can range from wondering how family relationships might be affected—by the revelation that a child is, in addition to being gifted, a member of a gender/sexual minority—to practical questions about how the child will be able to navigate school on a daily basis. This chapter will address general areas where these questions reside, with the goal of providing some guidance and reassurance to parents.

Child Development

Gifted children are children first. They need time to play, relax, explore, and make mistakes. They also often have insatiable appetites for knowledge, asking questions constantly. Many of them can, within the space of five minutes, inquire about micrometeoroids and then cry when someone else eats the last cookie. This behavior is referred to as asynchrony, which tends to fade as gifted children become gifted youth.[80]

However, the desire to absorb knowledge may not always be accompanied by the maturity necessary to process the knowledge obtained.[81] The reason that this concept is important for parents of youth who are both gifted and GLBTQ complex. People disagree on when kids become aware of their own sexualities, but people also commonly acknowledge youths' need to see their identities reflected in informational sources, curriculum, and intellectual mentors (whether accessed directly or via a body of work).[82] For example, educators know that students from different ethnic backgrounds benefit from seeing kids who look similar to them in books, as well as from reading about adults who share their diverse ethnicities and who have made significant contributions to society.

This holds true for gifted-GLBTQ youth, too. Where it gets complicated is where the desire for identity-affirming knowledge intersects with mature thematic material beyond the young person's ability to process. It is also not uncommon for gifted youth to ask questions about existence and the nature of being alive, including "Why me? Why am I different on so many levels?" Parents, who may yet be adjusting to the knowledge that their kid is not "straight," will nevertheless need to help their teen or pre-teen navigate these intersections. They need to do so in a way that supports the youth's developing identity in positive ways while honoring their level of maturity.

Academic Needs

Parents of gifted youth often find themselves spending a lot of time advocating at school to ensure that their kids get the appropriate levels of academic challenge and pace necessary to keep them engaged in learning.[83] When a child is also a member of a gender or a sexual minority, the scope of that effort expands. Not every lesson in every subject will need (or be able) to encompass all facets of the teen's identity, but parents should attempt to get teachers and mentors involved who will acknowledge and affirm the whole child. In doing so, they will send strong messages of love and support—not only about the child's intellectual abilities, but also about the teen's emerging adult identity. If parents and guardians do not provide this kind of support, gifted GLBTQ youth may struggle with self-esteem issues and question whether their parents accept them unconditionally.[84]

Safety Issues

Beyond addressing matters of visibility and intellectual engagement, parents may have to advocate for protection of their students' safety and fair treatment at school. According to the 2015 National School Climate Survey, conducted and compiled by the Gay, Lesbian, Straight Education Network (GLSEN)—GLBTQ students in America's schools continue to face hostility on a regular basis

- Almost all of LGBTQ students (98.1%) heard "gay" used in a negative way (e.g., "that's so gay") at school; 67.4% heard these remarks frequently or often, and 93.4% reported that they felt distressed because of this language.
- 95.8% of LGBTQ students heard other types of homophobic remarks (e.g., "dyke" or "faggot"); 58.8% heard this type of language frequently or often.
- 95.7% of LGBTQ students heard negative remarks about gender expression (not acting "masculine enough" or "feminine enough"); 62.9% heard these remarks frequently or often.
- 85.7% of LGBTQ students heard negative remarks specifically about transgender people,

like "tranny" or "he/she;" 40.5% heard them frequently or often.

- 56.2% of students reported hearing homophobic remarks from their teachers or other school staff, and 63.5% of students reported hearing negative remarks about gender expression from teachers or other school staff.[85]

Rules about issues from dress codes to bathroom use, from sports participation to names and gender pronouns to be used in the school setting, are in a seemingly constant state of flux. Parents can encounter many policy-based challenges that require advocacy, particularly for transgender children. Chapter 8 contains resources that may address these efforts.

Social and Emotional Needs

As they mature, most people develop the desire to feel like they belong somewhere, and gifted GLBTQ kids are no different in this respect. For these youth, however, finding others who are like them can be a challenge, especially in rural areas, where more traditional lifestyles tend to prevail. Developing social connections is another very important area in which parents need to invest some efforts.

There are organizations that exist to provide opportunities for highly intelligent people to meet each other in social settings. Mensa is one example of such an organization, and it has active programs for young people (in some areas of the country). There is no guarantee that joining a group that has been created for smart people will result in finding many other individuals who share other important attributes. However, clubs for smart people attract those who are also different in other respects. If a teen feels isolated because of being both gifted and GLBTQ,

34

finding a place where at least one of those elements is shared with everyone in the room can be life-changing in a very positive way. From there, other commonalities may be discovered, and friendships may form. Other types of programs where these youths might find a good fit include math clubs, fencing classes, and/or summer or after-school enrichment classes for advanced learners.

Many gifted youth are involved in the arts, such as music, visual arts, theater, or dance. These types of artistic engagement can bring not only creative satisfaction to gifted GLBTQ kids, they also provide places where these youth can find understanding friends. In addition, if a child has a passion for the arts, sometimes doing that endeavor and managing that activity's associated practices, rehearsals, learning of fingerings or lines, can give kids a much-needed sense of agency. This sense is particularly critical for youth who might otherwise feel as though life is happening to them in ways that are beyond their direct control, due to overexcitabilities.[86]

Parents will need to commit to providing opportunities for social interactions, even if doing so may take them out of their comfort zones or require driving and waiting times. Activities like these might not happen close to home, and if a teen does not drive or have access to public transportation or spending money, parents will need to provide transportation, entry fees, and an obvious desire to help their kids participate. This level of parental involvement can be challenging, but it is critical that teens know that their parents are supportive and willing to do what is necessary to help them find community.

In addition to groups, many young people find emotional support in literature. This publication provides a list of resources that address the social and emotional needs and challenges often accompanying being gifted and queer. Because so many gifted kids love to read, books can constitute an important and readily available source of knowledge, insight, and comfort to young people who may be adjusting to being different on two fronts.

Parents need to be aware that youth who identify as GLBTQ have increased risks for attempting suicide; in fact, they are twice as likely to attempt suicide as their heterosexual peers.[87] Often, gifted youth experience the world around them on a profound level, hearing every sound, feeling every touch intensely, sharing in others' joy or loss, and being moved by things that go unnoticed by other people. As parents, it can be difficult to know where and when this sensitivity to stimuli goes from allowing the child to fully appreciate her/his surroundings to being a painful experience. Attention to reactions, unconditional love, support, advocacy at school (especially if bullying is occurring), and willingness to talk openly will promote positive self-images and good mental health in kids. These factors will also create a safe environment where everyone feels valued and able to ask for help when needed.

Challenges in Providing this Guidance

Guiding these children takes significant energy. Most parents are not prepared for the demands that accompany raising gifted children, so they must invest real effort in learning about their kids' needs. When the gender-sexuality piece is added, even more commitment is called for, making self-care crucial for parents so they stay strong.

In each of the areas above, parents may find themselves frustrated by lack of the information they need to do a good job of parenting. Below are example challenges and approaches to addressing those challenges, from each category. The Resources chapter of this book is a place to look for further details.

Intellectual and Academic

Parenting challenges in this area include:

- Understanding the characteristics of giftedness
- Developing effective academic advocacy skills
- Learning what rights students have to academic acceleration and to inquiry into sexual-minority topics, as well as into the ways in which schools are obligated to support those rights
- Finding out what academic programs might be suitable for your teen

Often, people who do not specialize in working with gifted children, including friends and family, can be difficult to convince of the specific needs of this population, especially when sexual-minority status is part of a youth's identity. School policies can sometimes be particularly difficult for transgender students, despite direction from the U.S. Department of Education.

Here are some suggestions for parents dealing with these general challenges:

- Read extensively materials by specialists in gifted education and giftedness.
- Learn about local state and district policies on identification and acceleration.
- Find opportunities for enrichment at home and through local after-school programs.
- Connect with organizations for parents and educators of gifted students.

Social and Emotional

Isolation is one of the biggest challenges faced by gifted-GLBTQ kids and their families. Parents can feel helpless sometimes, seeing their kids feel alone and misunderstood. Other parental and youth challenges in this area include:

- Concerns about mental health and self-image resulting from feeling different.
- Overexcitabilities and how they might be managed and used to advantage.
- Lack of access to activities where similar youth may be found.
- Higher incidence of suicidality among non-heterosexual/gender-non-conforming youth.[88]

Suggestions for these challenges include:

- Delve into the research surrounding overexcitabilities.
- Explore the SENG (Social and Emotional Needs of the Gifted) website and publications.
- Engage in conscious efforts to maintain open communications in the home.
- Join an organization like Parents and Friends of Lesbians And Gays (PFLAG).
- Become familiar with signs that children may need active interventions to prevent self-harm.

Conclusion

Parents can, and should, explore any and all avenues that will allow their children access to enriching, soul-satisfying activities. For many of these kids, their awareness of their differences—especially of their being twice-different (gifted and GLBTQ)—will generate myriad challenges.

Parents need to do their research and be willing to expand their own horizons, so that they can meet these challenges with intelligence and love.

COMMUNITY MENTORING FOR GLBTQ GIFTED YOUTH

Teresa Manzella

One of the most important and rewarding activities in which parents and other family members of gifted GLBTQ youth can engage is networking in the community. This activity can consist of connecting with others who are facing the same challenges. Such networking can also include consulting with those who have already faced those challenges and who can provide much-needed wisdom for managing problems.

Because the gifted-GLBTQ combination does not represent a large percentage of the population, finding others who have this specific, shared experience can be difficult. This chapter includes ideas on possible networking opportunities. Some opportunities will be just for gifted children, others will be just for children who are GLBTQ, and yet others will be for both.

Intellectual and Academic

In most communities, there are clubs, classes, and volunteering opportunities that can provide intellectual stimulation and academic enrichment.

Parents and children should research available options together. Considerations when pursuing classes and other activities include:

- Location—How convenient is the activity?
- Cost—Are refunds available if the activity is not a good fit?
- Age/grade restrictions—Are those limitations flexible for gifted youth?

- Gender-based participation—Does a participant's gender matter for the program? Are the activity's planners open to transgender kids?
- Time commitment—How will the activity fit with other scheduled requirements?
- Parent involvement—Do parents?

Often, gifted children who meet through shared academic interests can form valuable, life-long friendships. When parents are also involved and share their challenges with other parents, they, too, can form friendships and gain useful insights that help them to be more effective as parents of gifted youth.[89] The specialists who teach or run the activities can become important mentors and contacts for parents and students going forward.

The internet also offers a rich variety of intellectual and academic resources—often at no cost. Massive Open Online Courseware (MOOC) is becoming available from an increasing number of universities. Lessons and whole courses can be accessed from the convenience of home. Some online learning programs also have community elements that connect students engaged in the same courses. Naturally, exercising basic precautions around personal information and network security are essential, but MOOC options provide higher-level instruction for children ready for the advanced content.

Finding academic mentors who are both gifted and GLBTQ can be a tough goal to attain. But a child who can identify with an intellectual mentor—one comfortable with the whole child—can feel connected in an important way. Since gifted children often feel more comfortable sharing ideas with adults, relationships with mentors can also be beneficial in reducing isolation.

Social and Emotional

Finding enriching intellectual/academic activities can satisfy some elements of a gifted child's needs, but there may not always be a positive social-emotional component. This area is one of the most challenging for gifted people in general, and it can be particularly so for gifted GLBTQ youth. Organizations that offer opportunities include:

- Gay Straight Alliances (GSAs)—Established at many middle and high schools, these groups provide safe spaces for students to socialize and plan events together.[90]
- Organizations for gifted children and/or families—National Association for Gifted Children and Mensa are two examples, which also have GLBTQ Special Interest Groups.
- Local organizations for parents and/or educators of gifted youth—The makeup of these organizations and the levels of activity can vary significantly from state to state.
- Local groups for GLBTQ families—These can be either offshoots of larger organizations or meetings started and run by a family trying to bring others together. Transforming Families, which exists to provide resources for families with transgender kids, is one example.
- Community centers for GLBTQ youth – These are often found in larger metropolitan areas and typically offer safe spaces for GLBTQ youth to congregate, have discussion groups, and receive counseling.[91]

Online chat groups—These can offer the opportunity to discuss concerns that might be difficult to share with parents or teachers, though security is essential, TrevorChat is a service that has moderated chat rooms to prevent cyberbullying.

Although just one of these groups has options in place specifically for gifted GLBTQ individuals, the connections made in these groups may lead to strong relationships. If the group and venue are large enough, the odds of one gifted GLBTQ kid meeting another one increase, and there might be a chance that one of the instructors/mentors is also gifted and GLBT. Whatever the size or nature of the activity, however, parents and teens need to make certain that an environment of respect and safety is supported.

Challenges in Providing this Guidance

As discussed throughout this chapter, community organizations that specifically offer connections with others who are both gifted and GLBTQ are quite rare. On a national level, Mensa and NAGC have GLBTQ groups, but these are largely geared toward adults, and there is little activity in the local areas where families can connect for events. Two of the greatest challenges in making community mentoring connections include: (a) protecting the safety of the young person and (b) maintaining the reputations of adults who mentor.

Safety of the student. Whenever minors are working directly with adults, caution is required to ensure that the situation is transparent. Most organizations dictate that children are not permitted to be alone with adults, however, in some situations this is not feasible. For example, private music lessons often do not include a parent being present. The presence of a non-student can be very disruptive to the pedagogical process. Families whose gifted GLBTQ kids need to take private lessons, or to meet with a professor one-on-one to conduct research, must be diligent about gathering information on the teacher, including getting a resume, checking references, and meeting for an interview prior to commencing lessons. Trustworthy mentors will have no trouble responding to polite requests of this nature.

Protecting the mentor. As difficult as it may be to acknowledge, GLBT adults who give of their time to work with young people can incur tremendous risk in doing so. With the persistence of the belief that young people can be "recruited" into non-heteronormative identities, the risks to mentors' reputations and livelihoods are real.[92] Parents, students, and potential mentors need to have honest, open conversations about the exact nature and scope of the mentoring relationship. Documenting those conversations and obtaining written agreements may seem burdensome, but those documents prove useful in ensuring all parties understand the mentoring relationship. Because every situation is different, all parties need to determine the best way to mediate the risks and build trust, so that the experience is a positive one for all those involved.

The advent of such tools as Skype can remove concerns for youth and adults regarding mentoring situations, as the interactions can take place in the virtual sphere. Such tools will never replicate the intensity of working directly together, but they are useful in some contexts.

Conclusion

Though finding the right fit for gifted GLBTQ youths in academic, social, athletic, and other areas takes dedication, the results have the potential to be life-changing. Finding others, whether they be students, educators, or adult mentors, who share interests and passions, creates a sense of belonging. These connections can help drive further development of skills and mastery, or they might result in a friendship. Mediating isolation is one the most important mentoring goals, one that has benefits far beyond the time spent engaged in specific activities.

FUTURE OPPORTUNITIES AND CHALLENGES

Terry Friedrichs

Both opportunities and challenges await gifted GLBTQ youth, as they move through their development trajectory. This chapter explores these opportunities and challenges in relation to their intellectual and social and emotional needs.

Intellectual and Academic Needs

As gifted sexual-minority students look for diversity at school, they may seek increasingly-varied school texts, speakers, and activities.[93] As these learners exercise their inquisitive sides, they may also experience gifted education curricula that increasingly values student research. Parents may feel more emboldened to ask questions about the possibilities for sexual diversity in school-based curricula and in independent student research. And community mentors, at least in some U.S. regions, may become more available for gifted GLBTQ teens' research projects and internships in the arts, history, health, politics, and science.

Gifted GLBTQ students and their parents and educators may be challenged, on the other hand, by states with "No Promo Homo" which prohibit GLBTQ-related discussions as "promotions" of sexual diversity. Parents in unsupportive locations are likely to feel as intimidated as their children when they inquire about their children's opportunities to learn about sexual-minority topics. GLBTQ-friendly community mentors, at some sites, may continue to be viewed as providers of "poisonous" ideas. And just as support may grow in some regions of the country for gifted transgender students, their parents, and mentors, other states and localities might clamp down, at least in the short run, on transgender-related classroom discussions, mentoring, and identity research.[94]

State and local gifted organizations may provide parents support for acceleration and grouping, as these parents advocate for these options in school for their children. And community mentors may find, especially at the end of GLBTQ learners' high school years, more students who wish guidance in their specialties when their schools have run out of sufficiently advanced curricula and mentors. However, some states and districts, supported by traditional educational philosophies and shrinking budgets, may continue to limit gifted GLBTQ learners' access to acceleration and to gifted student groupings. Parents may find it challenging to "go it alone". Also, gifted sexual-minority youth may not be able to access helpful community mentors if schools, in their quests to enhance students' testing achievement, require these students to remain on campus for longer periods. While some states may be amenable in the future to early and otherwise-varied forms of high school and college admission for transgender and sexual-minority students, other states may remain fixed in their policies.

Social and Emotional Needs

In a society in which both teachers and youth will probably be more GLBTQ-accepting, gifted sexual-minority youth may have social futures in which they can be more closely embraced for their differences.[95] Conversely, these youth also may be better understood when they separate themselves from other students with whom they find themselves at odds. Parents may feel freer to advocate for gay-straight alliances in schools and to explain anti-GLBTQ school occurrences that may have led to their children's individualistic behavior. Mentors, operating in an atmosphere increasingly supportive of GLBTQ students, may feel that they can inspire these youth even if schools continue to be unsupportive.

Though diminishing, physical and verbal harassment at school will not disappear overnight. Parents may need to expend more time than they wish in protecting their children from attacks. GLBTQ-friendly mentors, as in days of old, may need to band together to voice concerns about GLBTQ-related happenings in schools, as opposed to teaching groups of gifted students exciting new things about sexual-minority related arts, sciences, and politics. Advocates for gifted transgender youth may especially need to balance the need for open support for these youth with the knowledge that some schools and communities may resent that openness.[96]

Emotionally, gifted GLBT youth may have greater opportunities to have class discussions regarding human sexual behavior patterns. They may also be better advocates for their independence, self-image, and parents and peer relationships. Educators may respond by producing increasingly open lessons. Youth may also inspire their parents to point out positive GLBT images at home. Similarly inspired by inquisitive students, mentors may be more likely to respond to student inquiries about mutually assisting the sexual-minority community.

However, gifted sexual-minority youth may continue to face significant obstacles from some school systems that wish them to ignore their own GLBTQ feelings. Educators who lacked training on sexual-minority learners may not know how to react to these youths' feelings and can frustrate parents in the process. In such environments, mentors may be seen as taking youth down a "GLBTQ path" rather than down a "highly academic path that recognizes students' sexual-minority nature." Advocates may need to be prepared for a mix of outcomes from educational and social systems that can seem, at once, to strongly support and sadly ignore the widely-varied needs of these youth.[97]

Physical and Athletic Needs

There has been an increase in opportunities for gifted GLBTQ youth to engage in school sports and physical activities.[98] Parents may be better positioned legally to obtain from administrators their children's rights to participate in activities as open sexual-minority students. And mentors may become more vocal about their own support of GLBTQ people and issues, a support that is so important in often GLBTQ-restrictive sports and outdoors activities.

Some sports and physical activities have been slower than others to evolve in GLBTQ-positive ways. Less accepting climates may continue to create, rather than reduce, student tensions. Parents of such children may continue to fight battles for their children's safety instead of enhancing these students' performances. And these youths' mentors may tie up teaching energies in concealing their GLBTQ-related support rather than in uplifting their learners. Advocates for gifted transgender youth may find themselves on the frontline of controversies as they strive hard for democratic opportunities for their children in that most seemingly American of arenas, sports. They may find that despite newly issued official guidelines,[99] they face entrenched opposition that sometimes resembles the gridiron.

Conclusion

There are potential future openings to address each area of student need. These openings may include curricula, activities, and accelerative programs to address intellectual and academic needs—including GLBTQ and straight student openness, greater access to GLBTQ openness in athletic opportunities, and greater access to alternative schooling for athletic opportunities. Teachers, parents, and mentors will be challenged, as they are today, to find appropriate community resources to meet these youths' needs. In the future, unlike the present, though, the challenges may be more to sort out which of the various available resources might best fit these increasingly-known students' needs.

RESOURCES FOR GLBTQ YOUTH

Teresa Manzella and Bob Seney

As society becomes more sensitive to GLBTQ issues, the importance of providing resources for sexual-minority youth, for their straight peers, for their parents, and for teachers and administrators is recognized. Within just the last few years, these needed resources have begun to appear in the marketplace. A quick Google search provides many important, significant, and varied websites that provide answers, support, information, and encouragement.

The resources included in this chapter provide a wealth of information and support, ranging from social-emotional topics, scholarship opportunities for gifted GLBTQ youth, educational policy resources, survival guides for kids and parents, and opportunities to network.

For Educators

The *G-Squared Youth Advocate* website, established and maintained by one of this book's authors, Teresa Manzella, contains books, articles, and website links related to gifted organizations, GLBTQ advocacy groups, and to other resources helpful to supporters of gifted GLBTQ children. The site is a clearinghouse of resources related to gifted LGBTQ people, and offers the opportunity for readers to explore a wealth of information from one location at http://gsquaredyouthadvocate.com/resources.html#educators

Classroom teachers and school administrators may want to purchase the *Gay, Lesbian, & Straight Network's (GLSEN) Safe Space Kits*, at http://glsen.org/safespace. The contents of these kits help teachers ensure that GLBTQ students know that there are safe places they can go within the school. Even if these students do not stop by an ally-identified teacher's classroom, just knowing they have allies can make a huge difference.

The National Center for Transgender Equality (NCTE) offers information for educators and students regarding the U.S. Department of Education's policies related to transgender students at http://www.transequality.org/schoolaction. This is an area of policy that changes frequently and varies by state and district. Educators are encouraged to consult the *NCTE* website whenever questions of transgender student rights arise.

For Parents

Parents play a key role as advocates for their children. Self-education through research, reading, and connecting with other parents will help prepare parents of gifted GLBTQ youth to be effective in supporting their children at home, at school, and in the community. Chapter 5, which includes advice and suggestions for parents, also includes parent-specific resources.

This is a Book for Parents of Gay Kids: A Question & Answer Guide to Everyday Life by Dannielle Owens-Reid draws on the authors' website dedicated to LGBTQ issues and personal experiences. They also incorporate parental questions and answers to these often asked questions.

Teresa Manzella's *G-Squared Youth Advocate* site http://gsquaredyouthadvocate.com/resources.html#educators has resources for parents and other family members.

Rainbow Rumpus, http://www.rainbowrumpus.org, is a magazine for youth with GLBT parents. The site also offers free, downloadable books, geared mostly toward pre-teens.

Transforming Family, http://www.transformingfamily.org, which was started in Los Angeles but has seen chapters open in other areas of the country, offers online resources and, in some locations, meetings for transgender youth and their families.

For Gifted GLBTQ Students

In *It Gets Better: Coming Out, Overcoming Bullying, and Creating a Life Worth Living* edited by Dan Savage and Terry Miller, GLBT letter-writers tell their coming-out stories and talk about suicidal feelings and current challenges and accomplishments, while straight religious and political figures add their own encouraging messages.

Queer: The Ultimate LGBT Guide for Teens by Kathy Belge, Marke Biescheke, and Christian Robinson, provides a funny and humorous guide to support LBGT teens as they come out to their family and friends. The text also suggests ways to combat bigotry and homophobia.

Rita Mae Brown's *Rita Will: Memoir of a Literary Rabble-Rouser,* illustrates the author's life journey as a gifted-queer woman, emphasizing the importance of being true to one's self and the necessity of developing resiliency to counter discriminatory attitudes.

GLBTQ: The Survival Guide for Queer & Questioning Teens (2nd ed.) by Kelly Huegel, provides a wealth of useful information for LGBTQ youth on topics ranging from family life to school to romantic relationships.

Mellow Out They Say. If Only I Could by Michael Piechowski is suitable for gifted LGBTQ young adults, as well as their parents and teachers. It explores the nature of giftedness through the lens of Kazimierz Dabrowski's theory of positive disintegration, and explains how overexcitabilities can play significant roles in the lived experiences of gifted people.

American Mensa, Ltd., http://www.us.mensa.org, is part of the international high-IQ society. The society offers online forums, scholarships, and opportunities to socialize. The Gay SIG (Special Interest Group) is one of the longest-running SIGs in American Mensa.

According to its website, the *Gay, Lesbian & Straight Education Network GLSEN*, http://glsen.org/safespace, *"works with educators, policy makers, community leaders and students on the urgent need to address anti-LGBT behavior and bias in schools."* The organization conducts periodic surveys of LGBTQ youth experiences in school, the results of which are published roughly every two years.

Hoagies Gifted, http://www.hoagiesgifted.org, includes information on gifted education and 2e (twice-exceptional) issues, and has reading lists for gifted teens.

An organization that examines human rights issues throughout the world and in the United States, *Human Rights Watch* has published seminal research on the roles of educators and administrators in maintaining hostile school environments for LGBTQ youth. "US: Hatred in the Hallways" provides an illustration of how queer youth are treated in US schools https://www.hrw.org/news/2010/10/01/us-hatred-hallways.

The website for *Lambda Legal,* http://www.lambdalegal.org/know-your-rights/youth, has a large section dedicated to helping young GLBTQ people know their rights.

Because youth are coming out at ever-earlier ages, the *National Gay and Lesbian Task Force* http://www.thetaskforce.org, has established content and programming that is specifically geared toward young people.

Also in the Minneapolis-St. Paul area, *Quatrefoil Library*, https://www.qlibrary.org, has books suitable for young readers and coming-out resources, some of which are referenced online.

Reclaim, http://www.reclaim-lgbtyouth.org, facilitates access to mental health support, so GLBTQ youth may reclaim their lives from oppression.

Transforming Family http://www.transformingfamily.org, started in Los Angeles and now has chapters across the country, offers online resources and, in some locations, meetings for transgender youth and their families.

The *Trevor Project* http://www.thetrevorproject.org, is one of the leading organizations to offer crisis intervention and suicide prevention to GLBTQ community.

A related social networking site, *TrevorSpace,* https://www.trevorspace.org, serves lesbian, gay, bisexual, transgender and questioning youth, ages 13–24, and their friends and allies. The space is safe and moderated.

A long-standing organization, *Parents and Friends of Lesbians and Gays (PFLAG)*, https://www.pflag.org, provides resources and support for parents, families, and friends of GLBTQ people.

As one of the later groups in the GLBTQ community to be officially recognized in their search for open, supportive policies, transgender people have encountered legislative and social-conservative backlash that complicates advocacy strategies. This is an area that needs monitoring and timely research, for the latest in rules and regulations. Lambda

Legal, the NCTE, and Transforming Families are all sites that readers should check whenever questions arise.

*Please note that the appearance of these links in this publication does not indicate NAGC's endorsement of the materials found on the listed sites.

A Final Word

As mentioned earlier, organizational web content is continually expanding. While current when published, these links will eventually become a partial selection of what is available.

The evolution of attitudes can take a long time. The resources provided here are offered to help a wide variety of individuals—and regardless of where they are along their journey. We hope that they may continue to find such information and organizations invaluable for years to come.

ENDNOTES

[1] Kinsey, A. C., Pomeroy, W. P., & Martin, C. E. (1953). *Sexual behavior in the human male and female*. Philadelphia, PA: Saunders.

[2] Rosario, M., Schrimshaw, E. W., Hunter, J., & Braun, L. (2006). Sexual identity development among lesbian, gay, and bisexual youths: Consistency and change over time. *Journal of Sex Research, 43*(2), 46–58.

Sears, J. T. (2005). Introduction. In J. T. Sears (Ed.), *Youth, education, and sexualities: An international encyclopedia* (pp. 56–60). Westport, CT: Greenwood.

[3] Beemyn, B. G. (2005). Transgender youth. In J. T. Sears (Ed.), *Youth, education, and sexualities: An international encyclopedia* (pp. 864–868). Westport, CT: Greenwood.

[4] Kumoshiro, K. K. (2002). *Troubling education: Queer activism and oppressive pedagogy*. New York, NY: Rutledge.

[5] Sears, (2005).

[6] Sears, (2005).

[7] Borhek, M. (1979). *My son Eric*. Minneapolis, MN: Augsburg Press.

[8] Alyson, S. (2005). *Lavender lists*. Los Angeles, CA: Alyson Publications.

[9] Alyson, (2005).

[10] Sears, (2005).

[11] Beemyn, (2005).

[12] Peterson, J., & Rischar, S. (2000). Gifted and gay: The adolescent experience. *Gifted Child Quarterly, 43*, 430–444.

[13] Human Rights Campaign. (2014). Historical progress in states, cities, and school districts with GLBT-rights laws and guidelines: Maps. Retrieved from www.hrc.org.

[14] Friedrichs, T. P., & Etheridge, R. L. (1995). Gifted and gay—reasons to help. *The Association for the Gifted Newsletter, 17*(1), 4–5.

[15] Treat, A. R. (2006). Overexcitability in gifted sexually diverse populations. *The Journal of Secondary Gifted Education, 17*, 244–257.

[16] Gay, Lesbian, & Straight Education Network. (2013). *The GLSEN lunchbox: A comprehensive training program for ending anti-gay bias in schools*. Washington, DC: GLSEN.

[17] Human Rights Campaign, (2014).

[18] Sears, (2005).

[19] Treat, (2006).
[20] Human Rights Campaign, (2014).
[21] Sears, (2005).
[22] Davis, J. H., & Apuzzo, M. (2016, May 12). U.S. directs public schools to allow transgender access to restrooms. *The New York Times*. Retrieved from http://www.newyorktimes.com.
[23] Bernstein, J. (2017, April 1). My son, my daughter: A mother's evolution. *The New York Times*. Retrieved from http://www.newyorktimes.com.
[24] Gay, Lesbian, & Straight Educators Network, (2013).
[25] Sears, (2005).
[26] Peterson et al., (2000).
[27] Treat, (2006).
[28] Whittenburg, B., & Treat, A. R. (2008). Shared characteristics of gifted and sexually diverse youth. In N. L. Hafenstein, & J. A. Castellano (Eds.), *Perspectives in gifted education: Diverse gifted learners* (Vol. 4, pp. 140–176). Denver, CO: University of Denver.
[29] Friedrichs et al., (1995).
Friedrichs, T. P. (2012). Gifted GLBT youth: Counseling on pathways to freedom. In T. L. Cross, & J. R Cross (Eds.), *Handbook for counseling students with gifts and talents* (pp. 153–177). Waco, TX: Prufrock Press.
[30] Manzella, T. R. (2014). Home for the holidays: Reducing the stress for your gifted GLBTQ kids. *Parenting for High Potential, 4*(2), 2–3.
[31] Sedillo, P. J. (Under review). The 'T' is missing from gifted: Gifted transgender individuals: A case study of a female to male gifted transgender person. *Gifted Child Today*.
[32] Peterson et al., (2000).
Friedrichs et al., (1995).
Friedrichs, (2012).
[33] Friedrichs et al., (1995).
Friedrichs, (2012).
Hutcheson, V. H., & Tieso, C. L. (2014). Social coping of gifted and LGBTQ adolescents. *Journal for Education of the Gifted, 37,* 355–377.
[34] Friedrichs et al., (1995).
Friedrichs, (2012).
[35] Friedrichs et al., (1995).
Friedrichs, (2012).
Peterson et al., (2000).
Treat, (2006).

Whittenburg et al., (2008).

[36] Friedrichs, T. P. (2005). *Contextual social and emotional needs, and social and emotional teaching approaches, for gifted gay and bisexual male adolescents.* Ann Arbor, MI: UMI.
Hutcheson et al., (2014).

[37] Friedrichs et al., (1995).
Friedrichs, (2012).
Peterson et al., (2000).
Treat, (2006).
Whittenburg et al., (2008).

[38] Friedrichs et al., (1995).
Friedrichs, (2012).
Hutcheson et al., (2014).
Peterson et al., (2000).

[39] Friedrichs et al., (1995).
Friedrichs, (2012).
Treat, (2006).
Whittenburg et al., (2008).

[40] Friedrichs et al., (1995).
Friedrichs, (2012).
Treat, (2006).
Whittenburg et al., (2008).

[41] Friedrichs et al., (1995).
Friedrichs, (2012).
Treat, (2006).
Whittenburg et al., (2008).

[42] Friedrichs et al., (1995).
Friedrichs, (2012).

[43] Treat, (2006).
Whittenburg et al., (2008).

[44] Friedrichs et al., (1995).
Friedrichs, (2012).
Peterson et al., (2000).

[45] Friedrichs et al., (1995).
Friedrichs, (2012).

[46] Hutcheson et al., (2014).

[47] Sedillo, P. J. (2015). Gifted gay adolescent suicide and suicidal ideation literature research barriers on limitations. *Gifted Child Today, 38*(2), 114–120.

[48] Havighurst, R. J. (1972). *Human development and education* (3rd ed.). London, UK: Longman Group.

[49] Bucher, K. T., & Manning, D. (2005). *Young adult literature: Exploration, evaluation, and appreciation.* Upper Saddle River, NJ: Prentice Hall.

[50] Smetana, J., Campione-Barr, N., & Metzger, A. (2006). Adolescent development in interpersonal and societal contexts. *Annual Review of Psychology, 57,* 255–284.

[51] Kingore, B. (2013). *Rigor and engagement for growing minds: Strategies that enable high-ability learners to flourish in all classrooms.* Austin, TX: PA Publishing.

[52] Heacox, D., & Cash, R. (2014). *Differentiation for gifted learners: Going beyond the basics.* Minneapolis, MN: Free Spirit.

[53] Heacox et al., (2014).

[54] Friedrichs, T. P. (2014, Fall). GLBTQ curricula benefits all students. *Teaching for High Potential,* 9–10.

[55] Purcell, J. H., Burns, D. E., Tomlinson, C. T., Imbeau, M. B., & Martin, J. M. (2002). Bridging the gap: A tool and technique to analyze and evaluate gifted education curricular units. *Gifted Child Quarterly, 46,* 306–319.

[56] Alyson, (2005).

[57] Hunt, B., & Seney, R. (2009). Planning the learning environment. In F. Karnes, & S. M. Bean (Eds.), *Methods and materials for teaching the gifted* (3rd ed., pp. 37–70). Waco, TX: Prufrock Press.

[58] Silverman, L. (2013). *Giftedness 101.* New York, NY: Springer Publishing.

[59] Silverman, (2013).

Sommers, S. (1981). Emotionality reconsidered: The role of cognition in emotional responsiveness. *Journal of Personality and Social Psychology, 41*(3), 553–561.

[60] Sommers, (1981).

[61] Silverman, (2013).

[62] Recob, A. (2008). *Bibliotherapy: When kids need books: A guide for those in need of reassurance and their teachers, parents, and friends.* Bloomington, IN: iUniverse.

Seney, R. (2011, October). *Bibliotherapy: A gentle tool to help unwrap gifted adolescents.* Presentation at the Third Conference on Highly Gifted Learners, Denver, CO.

[63] Seney, (2011, October).

[64] Friedrichs, (2014, Fall).

[65] National Association for Gifted Children. (2015). *Supporting gifted students with diverse sexual orientation and gender identities* [position statement]. Retrieved from http://www.nagc.org.

[66] National Association for Gifted Children. (2009). *Nurturing social and emotional development of gifted children* [position statement]. Retrieved from http://www.nagc.org
[67] Sedillo, (Under review).
[68] Friedrichs, (2005).
Friedrichs et al., (1995).
[69] Treat, (2006).
[70] Outfront Minnesota. (2017). *Youth, transgender issues, and resources.* Retrieved from http://www.outfront.org
[71] Outfront Minnesota. (2017).
[72] Peterson et al., (2000).
Villaneueva, M. (2015). *We are "Fightin' Pigeons": Reflections on a high school for the arts nurturing gifted GLBTQ students. NAGC GLBTQ Network Newsletter, 3*(1), 11–20, Washington, DC: National Association for Gifted Children.
[73] Peterson et al., (2000).
Villaneueva, (2015).
[74] School Safety Technical Assistance Council. (2017). *A toolkit for ensuring safe and supportive schools for transgender and gender-nonconforming students.* Roseville, MN: Minnesota Department of Education.
[75] Peterson et al., (2000).
[76] Peterson et al., (2000).
[77] School Safety Technical Assistance Council, (2017).
[78] Friedrichs et al., (1995).
Friedrichs, (2005).
[79] School Safety Technical Assistance Council, (2017).
[80] Tolan, S. S. (2007). Giftedness as asynchronous development. Retrieved from http://www.stephanietolan.com
[81] Manzella, T. R. (2012). *Twice other: Cultural challenges faced by gifted and GLBTQ adolescents* (Master's thesis). Metropolitan State University: St. Paul, MN.

[82] Huegel, K. (2011). *GLBTQ: The survival guide for queer & questioning teens* (2nd ed.). Minneapolis, MN: Free Spirit.
[83] Davidson, J., & Davidson. B. (2004). *Genius denied: How to stop wasting our brightest young minds.* New York, NY: Simon & Schuster.
[84] Brown, R. M. (1997). *Rita Will: Memoir of a literary rabble-rouser.* New York, NY: Bantam.
[85] Gay, Lesbian, & Straight Education Network. (2016). *GLSEN 2015 National School Climate Survey: Executive summary.* Retrieved from https://www.glsen.org

[86] Piechowski, M. M. (2002). Experiencing in a higher key: Dabrowski's theory of and for the gifted. In M. W. Gosfield (Ed.), *Expert approaches to support gifted learners* (pp. 19–32). Minneapolis, MN: Free Spirit.

[87] Centers for Disease Control. (2017). *Lesbian, gay, bisexual, and transgender health.* Retrieved from http://www.cdc.gov/lgbthealth/youth.htm

[88] Peterson et al., (2000).

[89] Walker, S. Y. (2002). T*he survival guide for parents of gifted kids.* Minneapolis, MN: Free Spirit.

[90] Macgillivray, I. K. (2007). *Gay-straight alliances: A handbook for students, educators, and parents.* Binghamton, NY: Haworth.

[91] Huegel, (2011).

[92] Rofes, E. (1997). Schools: The neglected site of queer activists. In M. B. Harris (Ed.), *School experiences of gay and lesbian youth: The invisible minority* (pp. xiii–xviii). New York, NY: Harrington Park.

[93] NAGC, (2015).

[94] National LGBTQ Task Force. (2017). *Stay informed and on task force actions.* Retrieved from http://www.thetaskforce.org

[95] Friedrichs, T.P. (2007, Spring). Social and emotional needs, and preferred educational approaches, for gifted gay and bisexual males. *SIGnificance,* 3, 4, 7.
Peterson et al., (2000).
Whittenburg et al., (2008).

[96] National LGBTQ Task Force, (2017).

[97] Outfront Minnesota, (2017).

[98] Woog, D. (2008). *Jocks.* Los Angeles, CA: Alyson Press.
Griffin, P. (2005). *Strong women: Deep closets.* New York, NY: Harrington Park Press.

[99] School Safety Technical Assistance Council, (2017).

ABOUT THE AUTHORS

Terry Friedrichs led several NAGC's GLBTQ groups: its first, informal, educator-and-parent group (1992-1999), its Special Interest Group (2011-15), and its current Network (2015-17). He presently is the Network's Communications Secretary and an NAGC Leadership Development Committee member. He holds doctorates in gifted/special education and in educational organizing for GLBTQ and other underrepresented populations, and has fought successfully with others for LGBTQ-related Minnesota legislation for safe schools and equal civil and marriage rights. Terry has published over 20 scholarly pieces on educational needs and approaches for LGBTQ youth.

Teresa Ryan Manzella is a founding member of the NAGC GLBTQ Network, Past Gifted Youth Coordinator (2003–2017) of MN Mensa, member of the American Mensa/MERF National Gifted Youth Committee, and member of the NAGC Diversity and Equity Committee. Teresa holds a Master of Liberal Studies degree, the focus of which addresses the challenges facing youth who are gifted and LGBTQ, presents on this topic around the US, and has been published in NAGC magazines and other national gifted publications.

Robert Seney has served gifted LGBTQ students for more than 40 years as a secondary school administrator, gifted education professor, and researcher. He holds a doctorate in education and specializes in, among other areas, curriculum and bibliotherapy for gifted sexual and gender minorities. He serves as a Professor Emeritus at Mississippi University of Women and was named as "Mr. NAGC" by the NAGC GLBTQ Network in 2016 for his professional lifetime of work on behalf of gifted LGBTQ youth.

ABOUT THE EDITOR

Cheryll M. Adams, Ph.D. is the Director Emerita of the Center for Gifted Studies and Talent Development at Ball State University. She has served on the Board of Directors of NAGC and has been president of the Indiana Association for the Gifted and the Association for the Gifted, Council for Exceptional Children.

www.ingramcontent.com/pod-product-compliance
Lightning Source LLC
LaVergne TN
LVHW051528070426
835507LV00023B/3368